Developing French

French and English Word Book

Edited by Katherine Farris

Illustrated by Linda Hendry

A & C BLACK • LONDON

Published in 2007 by
A&C Black Publishers Ltd
38 Soho Square
London W1D 3HB
www.acblack.com

Text © 1991 Katherine Farris
Illustrations © 1991 Linda Hendry

ISBN 978-0-71-36-8514-5 (hardback)
ISBN 978-0-71-36-8513-8 (paperback)

First published in paperback in 2008.

11 10 09 08 07
10 9 8 7 6 5 4 3 2 1

A CIP catalogue record for this book is available from
the British Library.

Printed and bound in China by Leo Paper Products

This book is produced using paper that is made from wood grown
in managed, sustainable forests. It is natural, renewable and
recyclable. The logging and manufacturing processes conform to
the environmental regulations of the country of origin.

Tips for using the French and English Word Book

Exposing children to as much French as possible helps them to understand and communicate in the language. This word book contains hundreds of French words for everyday objects and situations. Children will love exploring the bright, detailed pictures and spotting words that they already know.

Read the words aloud so children can hear how they should be pronounced. Use opportunities such as getting ready for school, meal times and playtime to introduce and practise French vocabulary.

The colourful pictures are an ideal focus for question and answer activities, quizzes, puzzles and games to reinforce and extend children's learning of French. The large pages are ideal for paired work.

• Play counting, describing, guessing and finding games. For example, ask children *Combien de filles y a-t-il dans la classe?* (How many girls are there in the class?), *Quelle personne est grande?* (Which person is tall), *Quel animal est rouge?* (Which animal is red?) or *Où sont les petits pois* (Where are the peas?). Children can answer orally or point to the correct part of the picture.

• Try writing the French words from a page on Post-it notes or scraps of paper, and ask children to label different objects in a room or outside, remembering what they have learned from the word book.

• Ask children to point out nouns and verbs.

• To introduce and/or revise written and spoken vocabulary, cover up the labels and ask children to say or write the words in French.

• To revise grammar, cover up the labels and ask the child to tell you if they are masculine or feminine words.

Bienvenue chez moi
Welcome to my house

des tuiles
tiles

le toit
the roof

une chambre
a bedroom

une fenêtre
a window

le porche
the porch

un mur
a wall

le salon
the living room

le sous-sol
the basement

un perron
front steps

4

la cheminée
the chimney

la salle de bain
the bathroom

les escaliers
the stairs

une jardiniere
a flower box

la salle à manger
the dining room

le garage
the garage

une porte
a door

une corde a linge
a washing line

la cuisine
the kitchen

le jardin
the garden

un portail
a gate

une barrière
a fence

Voici ma famille
Here is my family

le grand-père
the grandfather

le cousin
the cousin (male

la cousine
the cousin
(female)

le père
the father

le frère
the brother

la mère
the mother

un bébé
a baby

un chien
a dog

la soeur
the sister

la grand-mère
the grandmother

la tante
the aunt

l'oncle
the uncle

la nièce
the niece

le neveu
the nephew

des jumelles
twins

un chat
a cat

la arrière-grand-mère
the great-grandmother

le arrière-grand-père
le great-grandfather

C'est le matin
It's the morning

se brosser les dents
to brush your teeth

prendre un bain
to take a bath

dormir
to sleep

lire
to read

s'asseoir
to sit

faire frire un oeuf
to fry an egg

manger
to eat

boire
to drink

tondre la pelouse
to mow the lawn

arroser les plantes
to water the plants

se battre
to fight

monter les escaliers
to go up the stairs

prendre une douche
to take a shower

se sécher les cheveux
to dry your hair

repasser
to iron

marcher
to walk

tomber
to fall

pleurer
to cry

rire
to laugh

regarder la télévision
to watch television

descendre les escaliers
to go down the stairs

Bonjour!
Good morning!

un blouson
a jacket

un chapeau
a hat

une chemise
a shirt

des bottes
boots

des chaussures
shoes

des chaussettes
socks

un peignoir
a bathrobe

des lacets
shoelaces

une robe
a dress

des chaussures de sport
trainers

une culotte
underpants

un sweatshirt
a sweatshirt

un maillot de corps
a vest

un tee-shirt
a T-shirt

une jupe
a skirt

un short
shorts

un pantalon
a pair of trousers

une chemise de nuit
a nightgown

un pullover
a pullover

un gilet
a waistcoat

un bonnet en laine
a woolly hat

un pyjama
pyjamas

des gants
mittens

une écharpe
a scarf

des pantoufles
slippers

un manteau
a coat

une ceinture
a belt

Mon corps
My body

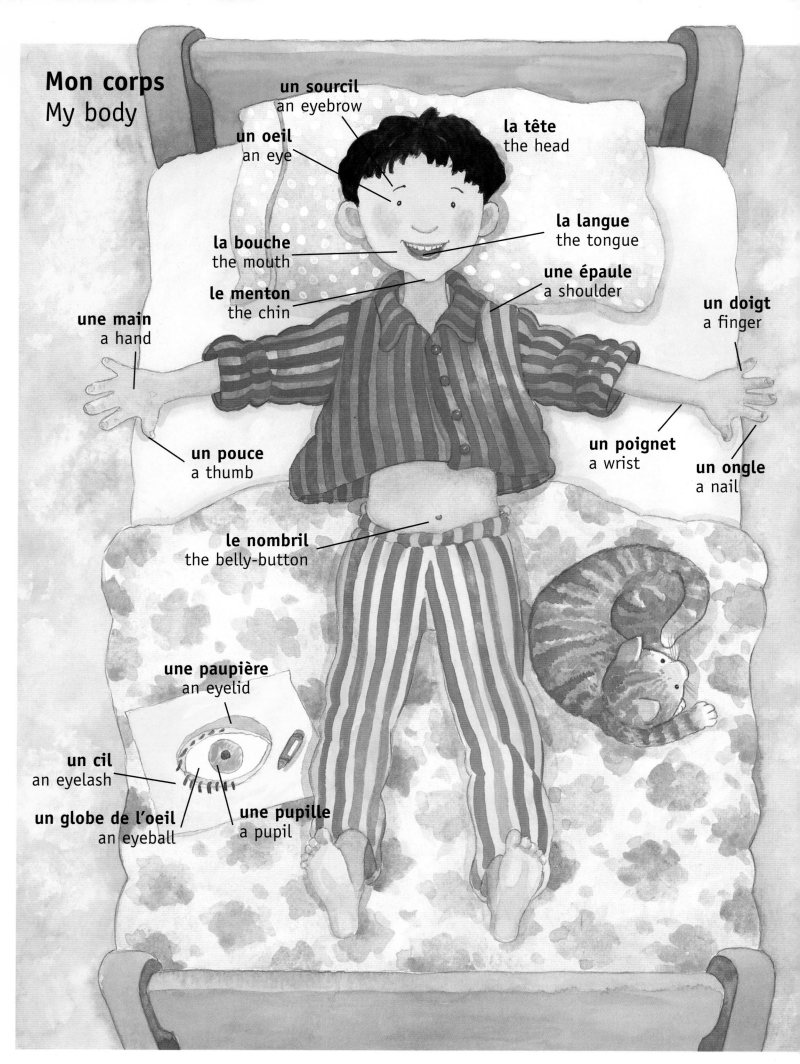

un sourcil
an eyebrow

la tête
the head

un oeil
an eye

la langue
the tongue

la bouche
the mouth

une épaule
a shoulder

le menton
the chin

un doigt
a finger

une main
a hand

un pouce
a thumb

un poignet
a wrist

un ongle
a nail

le nombril
the belly-button

une paupière
an eyelid

un cil
an eyelash

un globe de l'oeil
an eyeball

une pupille
a pupil

les yeux
the eyes

les cheveux
hair

les cheveux bruns
dark hair

une joue
a cheek

une oreille
an ear

les cheveux blonds
blond hair

le nez
the nose

une dent
a tooth

les cheveux roux
red hair

le cou
the neck

un coude
an elbow

le dos
the back

un bras
an arm

un genou
a knee

une jambe
a leg

un orteil
a toe

un pied
a foot

une cheville
an ankle

On déjeune
Breakfast time

un couteau
a knife

une assiette
a plate

une fourchette
a fork

une cuillère
a spoon

du beurre
butter

des croissants
croissants

une tasse
a cup

un oeuf
an egg

du sucre
sugar

du pain grillé
toast

une théière
a teapot

un grille-pain
a toaster

14

du lait
milk

un verre de lait
a glass of milk

un yaourt
a yogurt

une banane
a banana

des fraises
strawberries

du jus d'orange
orange juice

un pichet
a jug

des céréales
cereal

une pomme
an apple

un bol
a bowl

un sandwich
a sandwich

du beurre d'arachide
peanut butter

15

A l'école
At school

1 2 3 4 5 6 7

un   deux   trois   quatre   cinq   six   sept

Hello
Bonjour
Hola

Buon giorno
Guten Tag

שלום
γειά σο
喂
こんにち

un tableau noir
a blackboard

le professeur
the teacher

un globe terrestre
a globe

un garçon
a boy

une fille
a girl

un microscope
a microscope

des livres
books

un aquarium
an aquarium

un poisson-rouge
a goldfish

un bâton
a bat

un pupitre
a school desk

des élèves
students

une cage
a cage

un livre
a book

un hamster
a hamster

une chaise
a chair

huit   neuf   dix

Bom dia
Goeden Dag
Goddag
Szerbusz

les planetes
the planets

une horloge
a clock

un calendrier
a calendar

une carte du monde
a map of the world

un lapin
a rabbit

une marionnette
a puppet

un piano
a piano

une guitare
a guitar

un bureau
a desk

le soleil
the sun

une poubelle
a rubbish bin

une trompette
a trumpet

un cartable
a school bag

une flûte
a flute

un tambour
a drum

des patins à roulettes
roller skates

un jeu
a game

un tambourin
a tambourine

Dans la classe
In the classroom

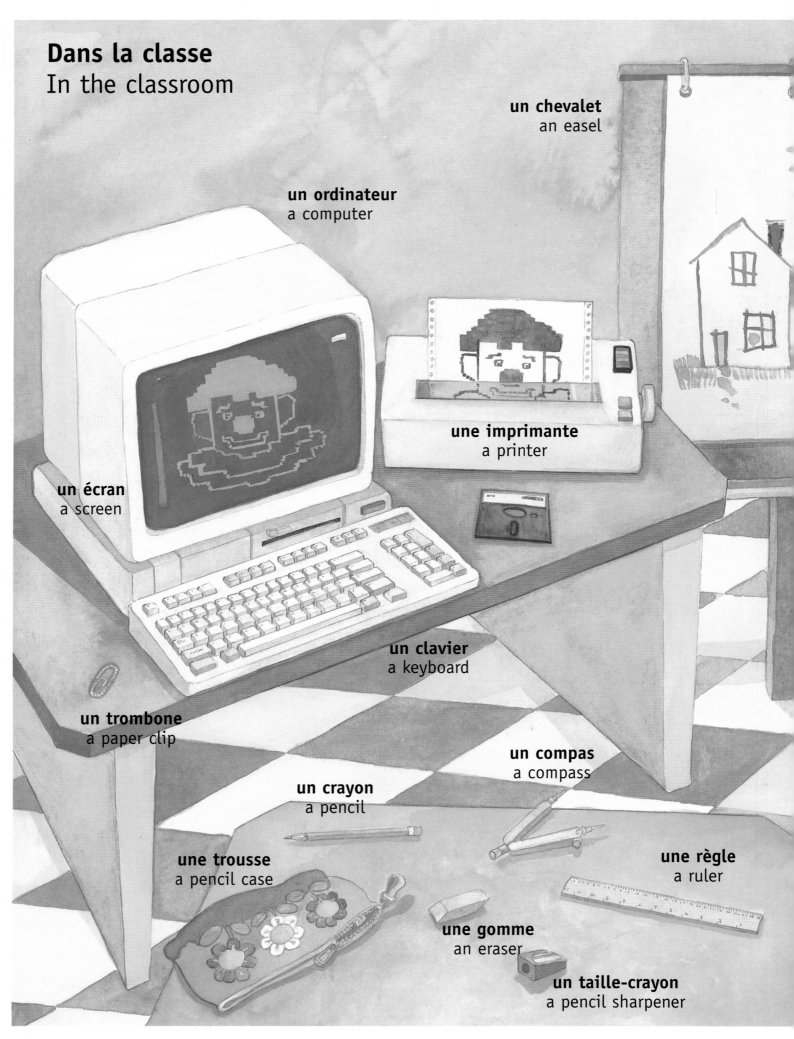

un chevalet
an easel

un ordinateur
a computer

une imprimante
a printer

un écran
a screen

un clavier
a keyboard

un trombone
a paper clip

un compas
a compass

un crayon
a pencil

une trousse
a pencil case

une règle
a ruler

une gomme
an eraser

un taille-crayon
a pencil sharpener

un dessin
a picture

un crayon de couleur
a pencil crayon

de la colle
glue

un pot de peinture
a paint pot

des crayons de cire
wax crayons

une boîte de couleurs
a paint box

un pinceau
a paintbrush

du ruban adhésif
sticky tape

des ciseaux
scissors

un dictionnaire
a dictionary

une calculatrice
a calculator

un stylo
a pen

un livre
a textbook

un cahier
an exercise book

Ce que je fais à l'école
What I do at school

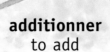

additionner
to add

donner à manger aux poissons
to feed the fish

soustraire
to subtract

compter
to count

étudier
to study

se balancer
to swing

jouer
to play

grimper
to climb

courir
to run

sauter à la corde
to skip with a rope

écrire
to write

peindre
to paint

dessiner
to draw

faire la sieste
to nap

En excursion
Going on a trip

un gratte-ciel
a skyscraper

des nuages
clouds

une ville
a city or town

un village
a village

une route
a road

un champ
a field

une rivière
a river

un bus scolaire
a schoolbus

un zoo
a zoo

un épouvantail
a scarecrow

une étable
a stable

un éléphant
an elephant

un cygne
a swan

une girafe
a giraffe

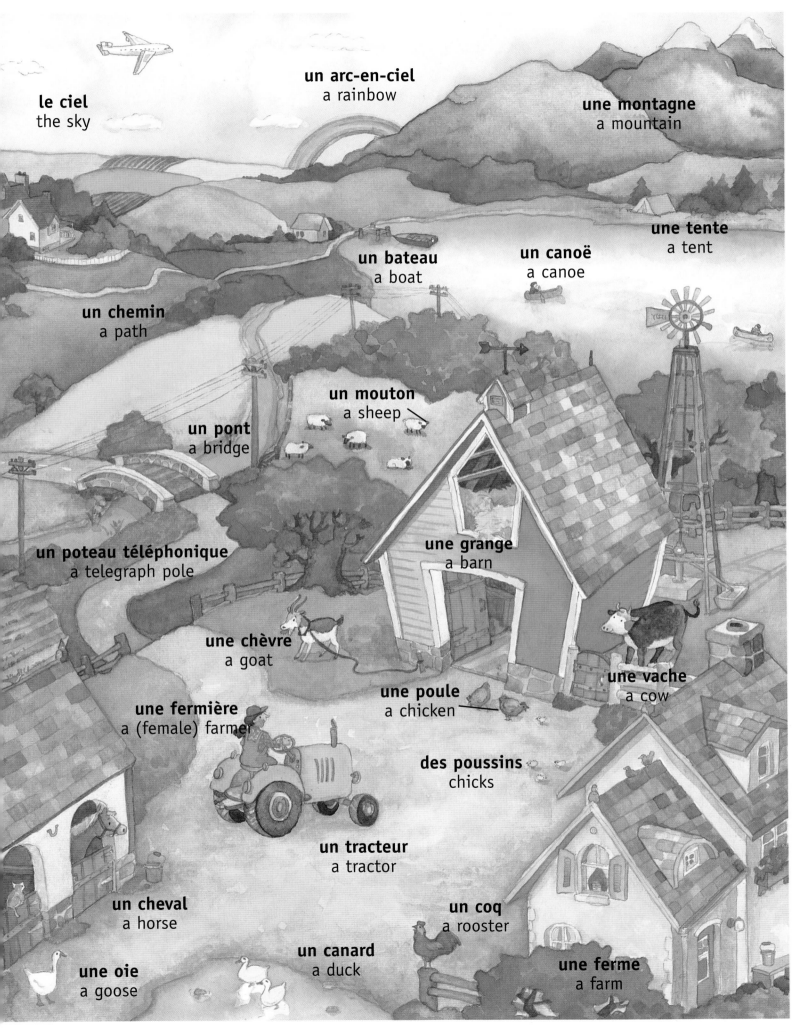

le ciel
the sky

un arc-en-ciel
a rainbow

une montagne
a mountain

une tente
a tent

un bateau
a boat

un canoë
a canoe

un chemin
a path

un mouton
a sheep

un pont
a bridge

un poteau téléphonique
a telegraph pole

une grange
a barn

une chèvre
a goat

une vache
a cow

une poule
a chicken

une fermière
a (female) farmer

des poussins
chicks

un tracteur
a tractor

un cheval
a horse

un coq
a rooster

une ferme
a farm

un canard
a duck

une oie
a goose

Au zoo
At the zoo

un évent
a blowhole

une nageoire
a flipper

un dauphin
a dolphin

une carapace
a shell

une tortue
a tortoise

un groin
a snout

un sanglier
a wild boar

un bec
a beak

un oiseau
a bird

une aile
a wing

une plume
a feather

une trompe d'éléphant
an elephant's trunk

une défense d'éléphant
an elephant's tusk

des bois
antlers

une queue
a tail

un cerf
a deer

un mouflon
a mountain sheep

une corne
a horn

un sabot
a hoof

des moustaches
whiskers

un croc
a fang

une crinière
a mane

une lionne
a lioness

le pelage
the fur

un ours polaire
a polar bear

une patte
a paw

une griffe
a claw

Mes animaux préférés au zoo
My favourite zoo animals

un chameau
a camel

un flamant rose
a pink flamingo

un phoque
a seal

un hippopotame
a hippopotamus

un buffle
a buffalo

un kangourou
a kangaroo

un pingouin
a penguin

un gorille
a gorilla

un serpent
a snake

un singe
a monkey

un toucan
a toucan

un ours brun
a brown bear

un crocodile
a crocodile

une souris
a mouse

un perroquet
a parrot

un lion
a lion

un tigre
a tiger

une baleine
a whale

En ville
In the city

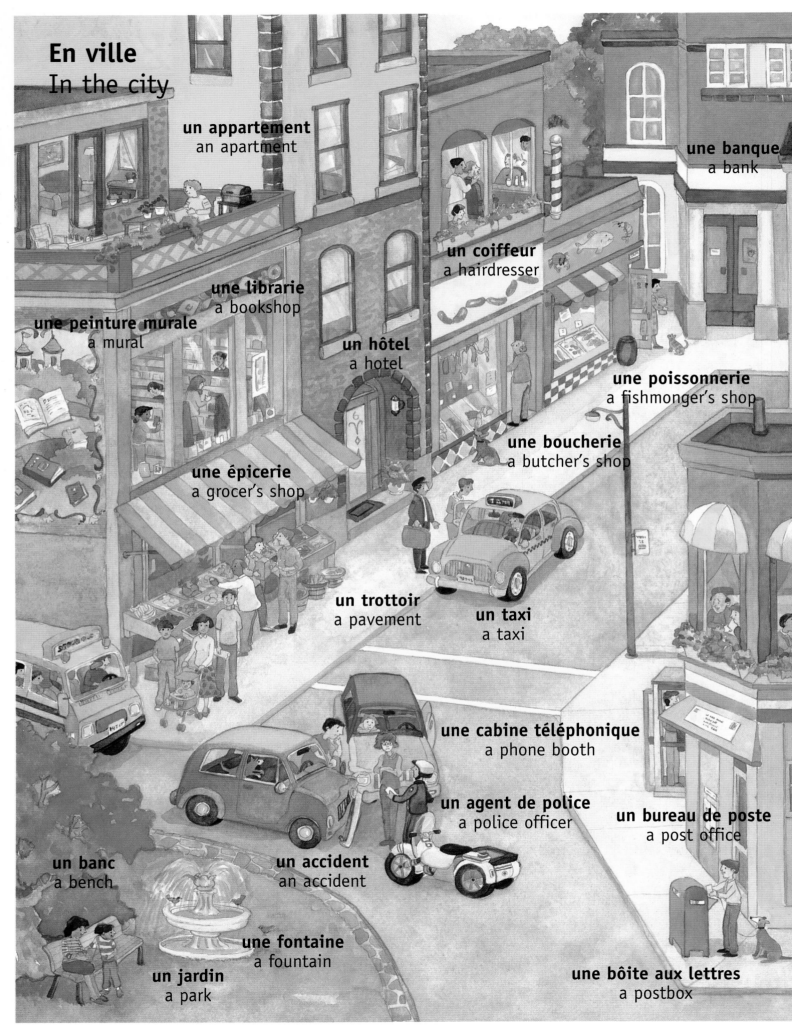

un appartement
an apartment

une banque
a bank

un coiffeur
a hairdresser

une librairie
a bookshop

une peinture murale
a mural

un hôtel
a hotel

une poissonnerie
a fishmonger's shop

une boucherie
a butcher's shop

une épicerie
a grocer's shop

un trottoir
a pavement

un taxi
a taxi

une cabine téléphonique
a phone booth

un agent de police
a police officer

un bureau de poste
a post office

un banc
a bench

un accident
an accident

une fontaine
a fountain

un jardin
a park

une bôite aux lettres
a postbox

28

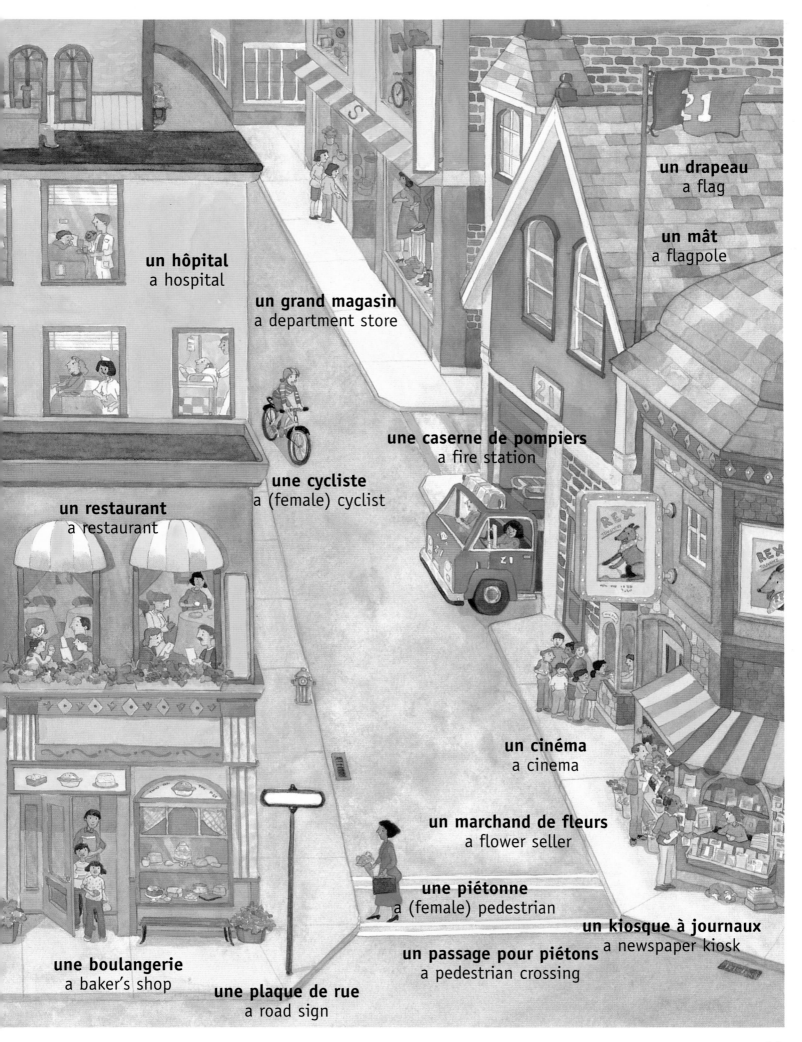

un hôpital
a hospital

un grand magasin
a department store

un drapeau
a flag

un mât
a flagpole

une cycliste
a (female) cyclist

une caserne de pompiers
a fire station

un restaurant
a restaurant

un cinéma
a cinema

un marchand de fleurs
a flower seller

une piétonne
a (female) pedestrian

un kiosque à journaux
a newspaper kiosk

une boulangerie
a baker's shop

un passage pour piétons
a pedestrian crossing

une plaque de rue
a road sign

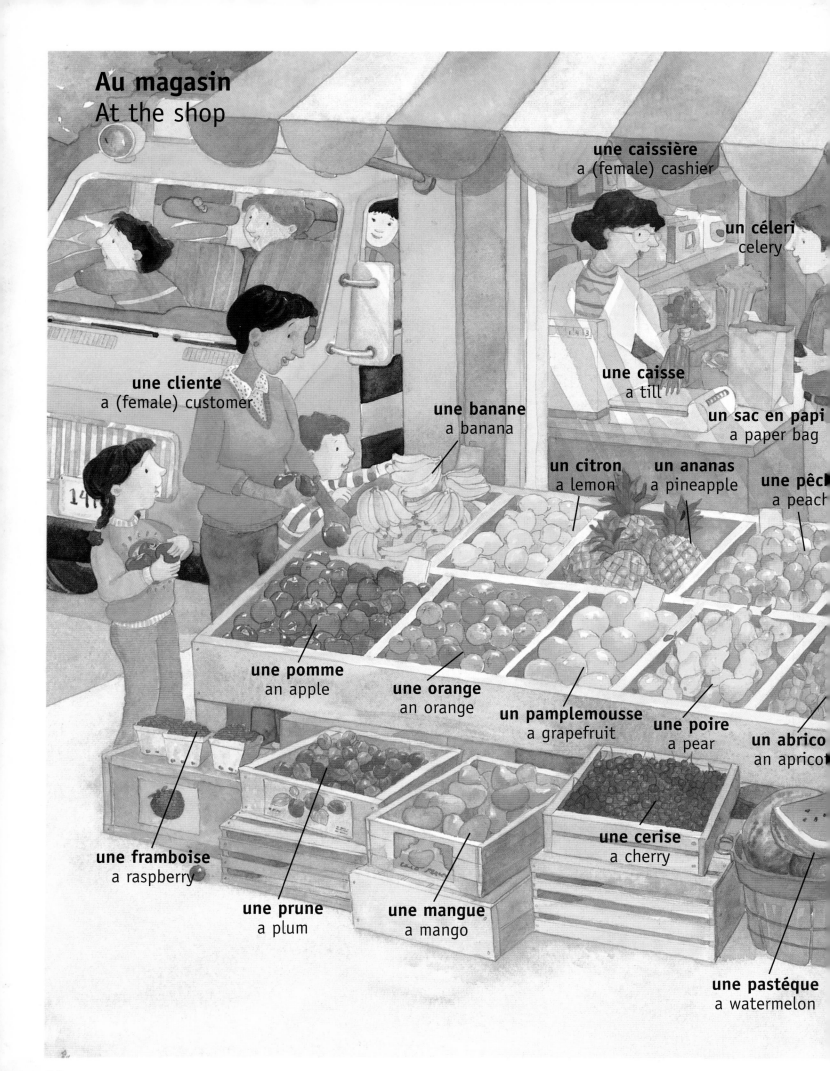

Au magasin
At the shop

une caissière
a (female) cashier

un céleri
celery

une cliente
a (female) customer

une banane
a banana

une caisse
a till

un sac en papi
a paper bag

un citron
a lemon

un ananas
a pineapple

une pêc
a peach

une pomme
an apple

une orange
an orange

un pamplemousse
a grapefruit

une poire
a pear

un abrico
an apricot

une framboise
a raspberry

une cerise
a cherry

une prune
a plum

une mangue
a mango

une pastéque
a watermelon

des raisins
grapes

un avocat
an avocado

des petits pois
peas

une laitue
a lettuce

un concombre
a cucumber

un épicier
a grocer

une tomate
a tomato

une carotte
a carrot

un oignon
an onion

une pomme de terre
a potato

du maïs
sweetcorn

des haricots verts
green beans

Les moyens de transport
Modes of transport

un hélicoptère
a helicopter

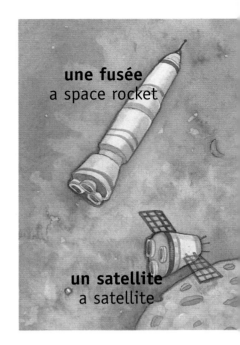

une fusée
a space rocket

un satellite
a satellite

une ambulance
an ambulance

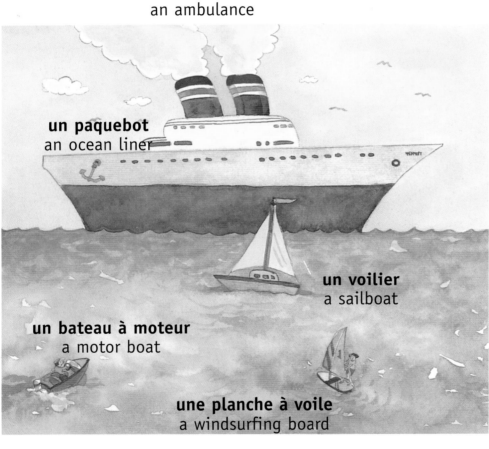

un paquebot
an ocean liner

un voilier
a sailboat

un bateau à moteur
a motor boat

une planche à voile
a windsurfing board

un tricycle
a tricycle

une voiture de sport
a sports car

une dépanneuse
a breakdown truck

un camion
a lorry

un avion
a plane

un autobus
a bus

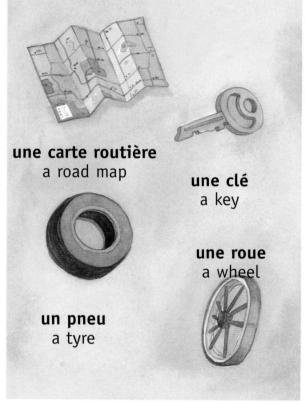

une carte routière
a road map

une clé
a key

une roue
a wheel

un pneu
a tyre

un train
a train

un vélo
a bicycle

un chariot
a wagon

un camion de livraison
a delivery lorry

une remorque
a trailer

un camping car
a campervan

Dans mon jardin
In my garden

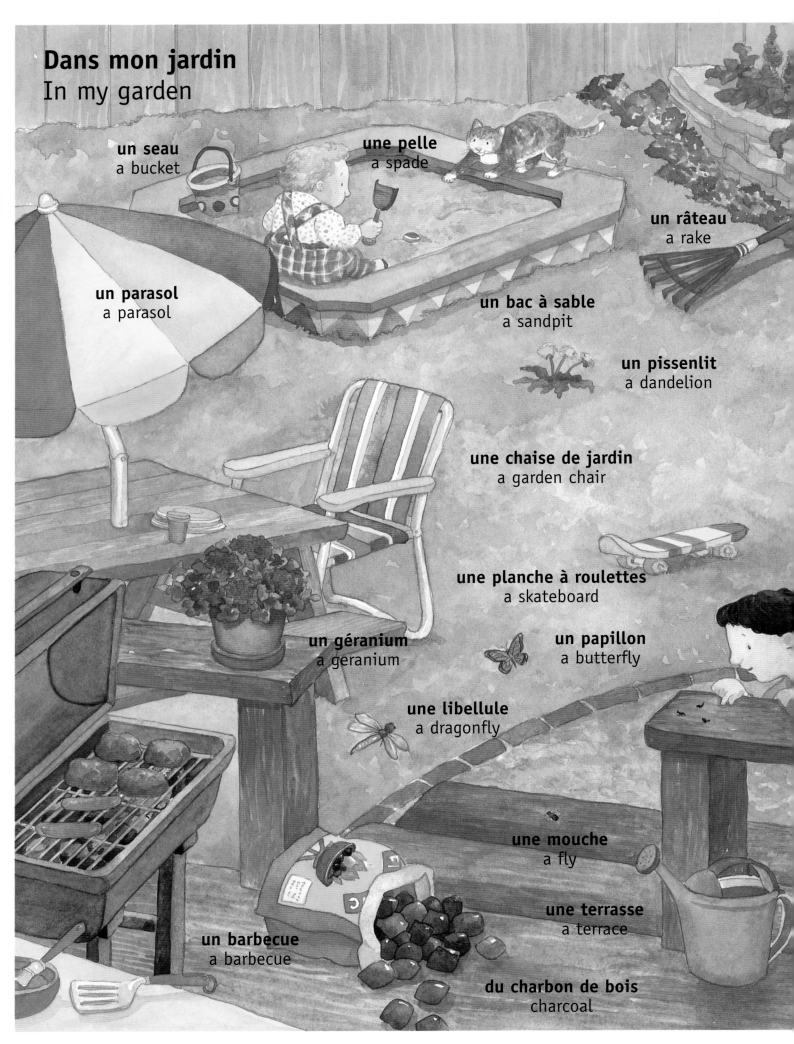

un seau
a bucket

une pelle
a spade

un râteau
a rake

un parasol
a parasol

un bac à sable
a sandpit

un pissenlit
a dandelion

une chaise de jardin
a garden chair

une planche à roulettes
a skateboard

un géranium
a geranium

un papillon
a butterfly

une libellule
a dragonfly

une mouche
a fly

une terrasse
a terrace

un barbecue
a barbecue

du charbon de bois
charcoal

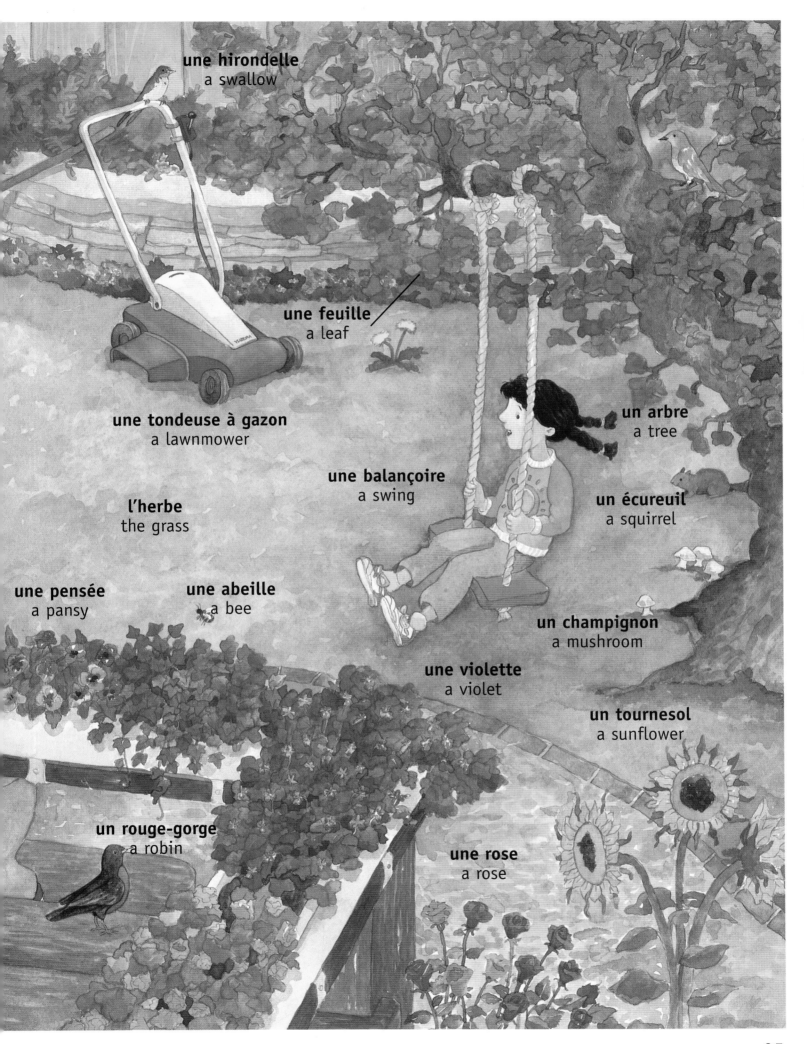

une hirondelle
a swallow

une feuille
a leaf

une tondeuse à gazon
a lawnmower

un arbre
a tree

une balançoire
a swing

l'herbe
the grass

un écureuil
a squirrel

une pensée
a pansy

une abeille
a bee

un champignon
a mushroom

une violette
a violet

un tournesol
a sunflower

un rouge-gorge
a robin

une rose
a rose

On mange du grillades
Barbecue time

des cornichons
pickles

un hamburger
a hamburger

des frites
chips

une nappe
a tablecloth

du fromage
cheese

du ketchup
ketchup

une tarte aux fruits
a fruit tart

une serviette de table
a napkin

de la mayonnaise
mayonnaise

de la moutarde
mustard

un plateau
a tray

du sel et du poivre
salt and pepper

des hot-dogs
hot dogs

une table
a table

de la glace
ice cream

des biscuits
biscuits

du gâteau
cake

une salade de fruits
a fruit salad

une corbeille de fruits
a basket of fruit

un jus de fruit
a fruit juice

une boisson gazeuse
a fizzy drink

une salade
a salad

Mes couleurs préférées
My favourite colours

rose
pink

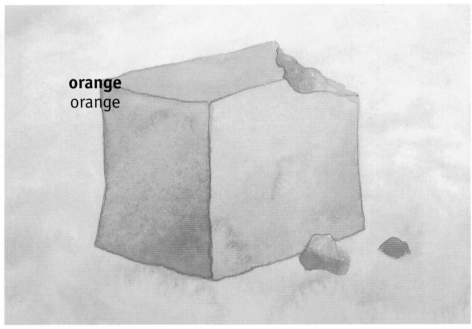

orange
orange

rouge
red

marron
brown

noir
black

vert
green

beige
beige

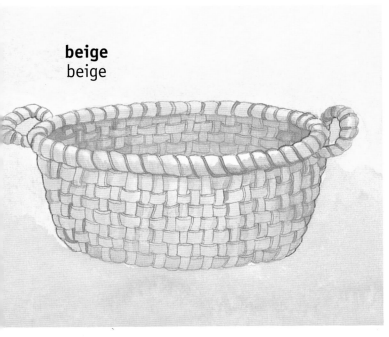

jaune
yellow

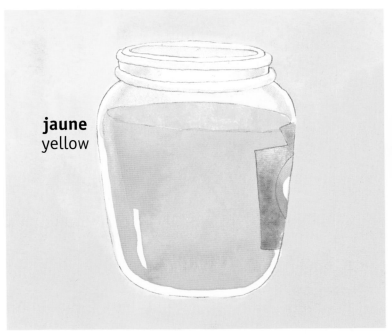

bleu
blue

gris
grey

violet
purple

blanc
white

De ma fenêtre
From my window

une étoile
a star

une maison
a house

une piscine
a pool

une échelle
a ladder

une pousette
a pushchair

une cabane dans un arbre
a treehouse

un trottoir
a pavement

la lune
the moon

un phare
a headlight

une voiture
a car

des amis
friends

une église
a church

une vasque
a birdbath

une chauve-souris
a bat

un arrêt d'autobus
bus stop

un bord du trottoir
a kerb

un nid
a nest

une rue
a road

une ombre
a shadow

un hibou
an owl

Bonne nuit!
Good night!

un store
a blind

un dessin
a picture

un vase de fleurs
a vase of flowers

les parents
the parents

une lampe
a lamp

un lit
a bed

un drap
a sheet

un réveille-matin
an alarm clock

une couverture
a blanket

un tiroir
a drawer

une commode
a chest of drawers

des oreillers
pillows

un tapis
a rug

une brosse à cheveux
a hairbrush

une chaise
a chair

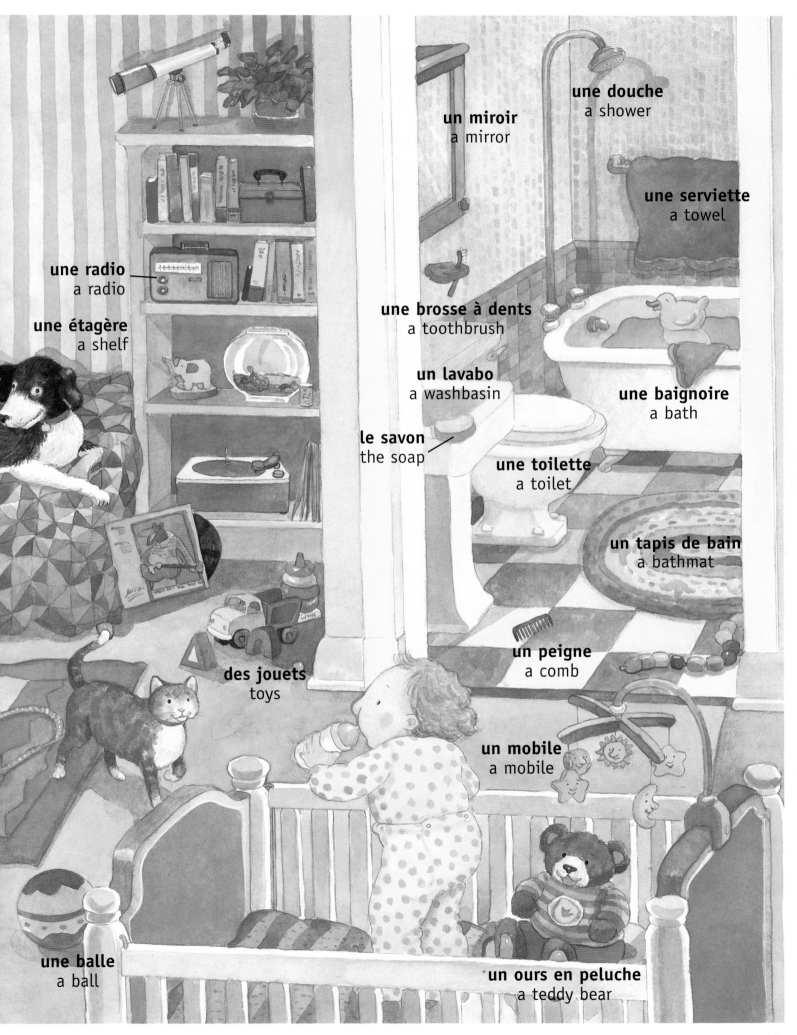

une douche
a shower

un miroir
a mirror

une serviette
a towel

une radio
a radio

une brosse à dents
a toothbrush

une étagère
a shelf

un lavabo
a washbasin

une baignoire
a bath

le savon
the soap

une toilette
a toilet

un tapis de bain
a bathmat

des jouets
toys

un peigne
a comb

un mobile
a mobile

une balle
a ball

un ours en peluche
a teddy bear

43

Quel est le contraire?
What's the opposite?

carré
square

rond
round

haut
high

bas
low

sur
on

sous
under

froid
cold

chaud
hot

plein
full

vide
empty

mou
soft

dur
hard

sec
dry

mouillé
wet

propre
clean

sale
dirty

ouvert
open

fermé
closed

grand
big

petit
small

heureux
happy

triste
sad

Word List

This is an alphabetical list of all the words in the book with their page numbers.

A

accident	28	blond hair	13	chips	36
add	20	blowhole	24	church	41
alarm clock	42	blue	39	cinema	29
ambulance	32	boat	23	city	22
ankle	12	book	16	claw	25
ant	34	books	16	clean	45
antlers	25	bookshelf	43	climb	21
apartment	28	bookshop	28	clock	17
apple	30	boots	10	closed	45
apricot	30	bowl	15	clouds	22
aquarium	16	boy	16	coat	11
arm	13	breakdown truck	32	cold	44
aunt	7	bridge	23	comb	43
avocado	31	brother	6	compass	18

B

baby	6	brown	38	computer	18
back	13	brown bear	27	corn	31
baker's shop	29	brown hair	13	count	20
ball	43	brush your teeth	8	cousin	6
banana	15	bucket	34	cow	23
bank	28	buffalo	26	crayons	19
barbecue	34	bus	33	crocodile	27
barn	23	bus stop	41	croissants	14
basement	4	butcher's shop	28	cry	9
basket of fruit	37	butter	14	cucumber	31
bat (animal)	41	butterfly	34	cup	14

C

bat (sports)	16	cage	16	customer	30
bathmat	43	cake	37	cyclist	29

D

bathrobe	10	calculator	19	dandelion	34
bathroom	5	calendar	17	deer	25
bath	43	camel	26	delivery lorry	33
beak	24	campervan	33	department store	29
bed	42	canoe	23	desk	17
bedroom	4	car	41	dictionary	19
bee	35	carrot	31	dining room	5
beige	39	cashier	30	dirty	45
belly button	12	cat	7	dog	6
belt	11	celery	30	dolphin	24
bicycle	33	cereal	15	door	5
big	45	chair	16, 42	dragonfly	34
bird	24	charcoal	34	draw	21
birdbath	41	cheek	12	drawer	42
biscuits	37	cheese	36	dress	10
black	38	cherry	30	drink	8
blackboard	16	chest of drawers	42	drum	17
blanket	42	chicks	23	dry	45
blind	42	chimney	5	dry your hair	9
		chin	12	duck	23

E

ear	12
easel	18
eat	8
egg	14
elbow	13
elephant	22
elephant's trunk	24
elephant's tusk	24
empty	44
eraser	18
eye	12
eyeball	12
eyebrow	12
eyelash	12
eyelid	12

F

fall	9
fang	25
farmer	23
father	6
feather	24
feed the fish	20
fence	5
field	22
fight	8
fin	24
finger	12
fire station	29
fishmonger	28
fizzy drink	37
flag	29
flagpole	29
flipper	24
flower box	5
flower vase	42
flower seller	29
flute	17
fly	34
foot	13
fork	14
fountain	28
friends	41
front steps	4
fruit juice	37
fruit salad	37
fruit tart	36
fry an egg	8